5 EASY WAYS TO DISCOVER HOT NICHES

Your Ultimate Guide to Navigating the Labyrinth of Markets and Uncovering Untapped Potential

Jolene R. Smith

1

TABLE OF CONTENTS

CHAPTER 1.. 6
CHAPTER 2.. 9
CHAPTER 3...11
CHAPTER 4.. 16
CHAPTER 5.. 19
CONCLUSION..25

INTRODUCTION

In a world brimming with opportunities, finding the perfect niche can feel like searching for a needle in a haystack. Yet, buried within this vast expanse of possibilities lie hidden gems waiting to be unearthed. Welcome to "5 Easy Ways To Discover Hot Niches," your ultimate guide to navigating the labyrinth of markets and uncovering untapped potential.

If you've been thinking about starting a new online business but have yet to do your research on the market, the principles and steps outlined in this book will help you know your niche thoroughly, so you can avoid wasting your time and money on trying to start an online business in an unprofitable niche.

Whether you're an aspiring entrepreneur, a seasoned marketer, or simply someone with a keen eye for spotting trends, this book is your roadmap to success. Drawing upon years of industry expertise and meticulous research, each chapter unveils invaluable strategies to identify lucrative niches effortlessly. From dissecting consumer behavior to leveraging emerging technologies, we delve into proven methodologies guaranteed to ignite your entrepreneurial spirit. Prepare to embark on a journey of discovery, where every turn brings you closer to your entrepreneurial dreams. Get ready to transform your ideas into thriving ventures as we unlock the secrets to finding your niche in today's dynamic marketplace.

CHAPTER 1

IDENTIFY YOUR PASSIONS AND INTERESTS

"Unleash your potential by discovering the passions that fuel your soul. Dive deep into your passions, discovering the realms that pique your attention. Listen to your heart's whispers and welcome the sparks that illuminate your way. In your search for hot niches, let your enthusiasm guide you to unexplored prospects. Explore upcoming trends, sectors, and markets with zeal. Combine your particular expertise with your passions to create a recipe for success. Fuel your journey with boundless excitement and determination. Remember that in the pursuit of excellence, passion is your most powerful ally. "Seize, own, and thrive!"

If you haven't already identified your interests and what you are passionate about, this is where you will want to start. Being in business for yourself is anything but easy, and at some point, you are going to be tested.

If you are running a business that you don't care about, your chances of quitting when things go bad grow dramatically. This is especially true if you are a first-time business owner.

This doesn't imply that you have to discover the perfect fit. You simply need to be passionate about some area of running a business.

Having even one part of the business that you are enthusiastic about increases the likelihood that you will remain with it, especially when faced with obstacles.

If you don't care about the topic, you may not be able to sustain the motivation that is needed to persevere.

The first stage is to list ten areas in which you are passionate or have a topical interest. If you are having trouble doing this, here are a few prompts to help you figure it out.

- What do you like to do in your free time? When you're not doing it, what kinds of things do you want to do?

- What kinds of magazines do you subscribe to? Are there any topics that you like to learn about?

- What clubs and organizations do you participate in?

CHAPTER 2

IDENTIFY PROBLEMS YOU CAN SOLVE

Once you've identified the things that you are passionate about, you can start narrowing down your options. If you want to develop a profitable business, you must first uncover difficulties that your target audience is experiencing, and then take the time to assess whether you can solve them.

Recognizing challenges to address is analogous to uncovering hidden treasures. It's about peeking into consumers' hearts and thoughts, recognizing their difficulties, and turning obstacles into possibilities.

Begin by immersing yourself in the lives of your target demographic. Listen carefully to their complaints, frustrations, and unmet needs. What keeps people awake in the night? What hurdles stand in the way of their goals? These are the hints that will take you to unexplored marketplaces ripe with opportunity.

Next, search for trends and patterns that point to developing difficulties or altering demands. Whether it's a technical gap, a sociological shift, or an underserved niche, keep an eye out for chances that others may have missed.

But don't only notice problems; become the solution. Use your creativity and intelligence to create products or services that target these pain spots with accuracy. Allow innovation to guide you as you streamline procedures, improve ease, or provide personalized solutions.

The most successful businesses in hot niches face problems head on and turn them into victories. So roll up your sleeves, delve deep into the ocean of unmet demands, and emerge victorious as the champion of your specialty.

If you're not sure how to approach this stage of the process, here are a few things you may do to assist you find difficulties in specific niches.

- Work with members of your target audience to get their input. Have one-on-one conversations with members of your target audience and ask specific questions that will help you to uncover specific pain points.

- Look at online forums. Get online and look for forums that are related to the niches that you are considering. Search through the discussions that are taking place. Try to determine common questions that members are asking and trying to find out what problems they are having.

- Conduct keyword research. Use the Google Trends and Google AdWords tools to experiment with different keyword combinations. Doing this can help you identify specific search terms that are related to pain points that your target audience may be experiencing.

CHAPTER 3

RESEARCH YOUR COMPETITION

Investigating your competitors is analogous to exploring the landscape before beginning on an adventure. It is about acquiring insights, comprehending the situation, and identifying chances that others may have overlooked.

Begin by identifying your immediate and indirect competitors, then look into their plans, strengths, and flaws. Analyze their products, pricing, marketing strategies, and customer engagement channels with the precision of a seasoned explorer charting new territory.

But don't stop there; dig deeper. Identify market gaps, or places where rivals are underserving or disregarding their target audience's demands. These voids are magnificent opportunities waiting to be taken.

Next, learn from their accomplishments and mistakes. What tactics drove them to the pinnacle of success? What pitfalls did they face along the way? Use these insights to plan your own journey, guided by the knowledge of those who have gone before you.

Armed with this knowledge, you're ready to build out your own market niche. Combine creativity with a thorough awareness of your competition to carve a route that is distinctively yours. Remember, in the world of hot niches, the trip is just as exciting as the destination. So, thoroughly research your competitors and allow your entrepreneurial spirit to fly to new heights.

Having competition isn't always a bad thing. If you find that the niche you are looking at has some competition, it may mean that you've found a niche that will be profitable.

However, you need to thoroughly analyze the competing sites to see if there is a place in the niche for another business. To start with, you'll want to create a new
spreadsheet and log all of the competing websites that you can find.

Next, you'll want to evaluate each site to see if there is still room for you to stand out from the crowd and develop a profitable business. You must decide whether or not you can still rank on Google using the keywords you have picked.

Figure out if there is still a way that you can differentiate yourself from the rest of the crowd and create a unique offer. Here are several different ways that you can enter a niche market and still find success even if there are already a number of sites that are serving the market.

- You can easily outrank your competition if their sites contain low-quality content. If other business owners aren't producing high-quality content that benefits their target audience, you still have an opportunity to develop a successful business in that sector.

- Many sites have a lack of transparency. Many new business owners have been able to radically disrupt whole sectors by developing a transparent and authentic presence in a market where other sites are deemed impersonal, overly corporate.

- If you've discovered a keyword that has a relatively high volume of searches, but little paid advertising or competition, there is an opportunity for a new business owner to upset the market. The lack of paid competition can create tremendous opportunities.

CHAPTER 4

DETERMINE THE PROFITABILITY OF YOUR NICHE

By now, you should have a solid sense of what niche you want to pursue. While you may not have completely narrowed down your list to a single topic, you've likely found a couple of ideas that you feel pretty good about.

Now you'll need to figure out how much you can potentially make in the specialty. A great place to start your search is Clickbank. Clickbank is a market platform for vendors to sell their digital products. It is the largest affiliate marketing network for digital products like software, eBooks, and membership sites.

You can use the site to browse the top products in your category. If you can't find any deals in a specific category, that's not a good sign. It could be a sign that no one has been able to monetize the niche. You want to locate categories that provide a sufficient amount of products but not an overabundance.

Make a note of price points while researching so you know how to price your own products to remain competitive.

You'll also want to keep in mind that you don't necessarily have to have a product offering of your own to start your business.

You can partner with a product's creator, advertisers, and site owners in your niche to start making commissions by selling their products while you work on your own unique solution.

A strategic study is the first step in unlocking the secrets of profitability in your area. Explore market trends, client wants, and rival strategies. Utilize the power of data analytics to identify lucrative opportunities. Evaluate the probable ROI of each investment precisely. Stay agile and quickly adjust to shifting landscapes. Create a distinctive selling proposition that distinguishes you. Use the power of creativity to generate appealing offers. With prudent financial planning, you can strike a balance between risks and rewards. Embrace continual learning to stay ahead of the competition. Remember that profitability is found at the convergence of passion, competence, and market need. "Seize the moment and thrive!"

CHAPTER 5

TEST YOUR IDEA

Now that you've gathered the necessary information to select a niche, all you have to do is put your idea to the test.

One simple approach to accomplish this is to construct a landing page for pre-sales of the product you're producing. Then you can use different advertising and marketing methods to drive traffic to your landing page.

If you don't get enough pre-sales, do become discouraged. You could still be in a profitable niche, but either your messaging isn't quite right or you haven't discovered the perfect offer.

You should begin to leverage A/B split testing, so you can optimize your conversions and determine whether or not there is anything stopping your target audience from taking action and buying your products.

Once you've determined that the niche you've chosen and the product you're offering is viable, you'll want to begin to develop a fully functioning website. You'll want to include a blog on the site, so you can begin to generate more traffic and boost your revenue.

You'll want to keep in mind that there isn't necessarily a perfect process for finding the perfect niche. You will need to complete your homework and go further.

If you find yourself stuck in the planning phase, you'll never get around to starting and won't find yourself on the path to success. As an entrepreneur, simply having a great idea isn't enough, you have to learn how to become a good starter if you want to be successful. In the thrilling search of uncovering hot niches, testing your idea is the furnace in which dreams become realities. It's where sparks of inspiration turn into raging fires of creation. To begin this journey, you must first embrace the spirit of experimenting by welcoming the unknown with open arms.

Imagine your concept as a raw gemstone that needs to be polished to perfection. Testing is the process of refining that jewel, chiseling away flaws until it shines brightly in the market's eyes. But how do you begin?

Begin by becoming intimately familiar with your desired niche. Engage with potential consumers, solicit input, and watch their reactions with the sharp eye of a master craftsman. Pay special attention to their pain points, ambitions, and goals. These insights will guide your entrepreneurial journey.

Next, turn your ideas into concrete solutions. Create prototypes, polls, or pilot programs to measure interest and collect real-world data. Embrace agility by iterating quickly in response to feedback and market developments. Remember that flexibility is the foundation of success in the ever-changing world of hot niches.

Prepare to face hurdles and setbacks while testing your idea. Accept them as opportunities for development and learning. Each difficulty you overcome puts you one step closer to turning your idea into a marketable masterpiece.

However, testing is more than just improving your concept; it also involves validating its practicality. Analyze crucial indicators like client acquisition cost, conversion rates, and profitability to ensure that your proposal is not just unique but also long-term viable.

Maintain your enthusiasm and purpose during this process. Let them be the driving forces that carry you onward, even when the waters of doubt get stormy. With unyielding drive and a tireless pursuit of excellence, you'll come out of the testing phase stronger, smarter, and ready to take on the world of hot niches.

In the furnace of testing, your idea evolves from a mere concept to a beacon of possibilities, demonstrating the power of invention and tenacity. So, kindle the flames of discovery, test your concept with zeal, and let it shine brightly in the constellation of hot niches.

CONCLUSION

Now that you've uncovered the secrets to discovering hot niches, it's time to put your newfound knowledge into action. Take the first step towards entrepreneurial success by identifying a niche that aligns with your passions and expertise. Dive deep into research, analyze market trends, and seize opportunities with confidence.

Don't let fear or hesitation hold you back. Start brainstorming ideas, refining your concepts, and laying the groundwork for your next venture. Whether it's launching a new product, starting a blog, or offering a specialized service, the possibilities are endless.

Remember, the journey to entrepreneurial greatness begins with a single decision to act. So, don't delay any longer. Take charge of your future, unleash your creativity, and embark on the exciting path of entrepreneurship today. Your dreams are within reach – all you have to do is take the leap.

Unleash your entrepreneurial spirit now! Identify a niche, dive into research, and take decisive action. Your journey to success starts today. Dare to make your mark!

www.ingramcontent.com/pod-product-compliance
Lightning Source LLC
Chambersburg PA
CBHW070241260726
48658CB00006BA/2388